MW01602171

© 2019

All rights reserved.

Unauthorized reproduction, in any manner, is prohibited.

When He Left…

Based on a true story

By: Denthia Wright

And we know that all things work together for good to them that love God; to them who are the called according to his purpose ~Romans 8:28

Kiss Lashanda for me Ma,

we miss all of you so much. We still have work to do….

I was sitting in a chair, my Therapist sitting right across from me with her legs crossed. Her name was Heather, Caucasian, early 30's. She sat there encouraging me to take all my medications as I should. Olanzapine was for sleeping. Buspirone was for the anxiety and Prozac was for the depression. For almost two years I had been taking these medications. I knew I needed help but when my sister passed away, I couldn't take it anymore. I needed someone to talk to other than family and friends. It was good that I had made the decision to do so. Speaking with Heather opened my eyes. It made me look at things differently. She'd explain to me how I should focus on everything positive and grasp whatever excited me. She always spoke about forgiveness. My mother spoke about the same. I guess they both could tell by the way I talked that I was hurting. That hurt had begun to take a toll on my body and mind. As soon as my session was over, I went home, showered and got in bed. I had to work at 11pm.

I'll never forget it. I was at work auditing the med-cart and as clear as day something spoke to my spirit saying, "He's going to leave you." I froze for a moment then quickly grabbed my phone off the top of the med-cart and texted my husband exactly what I had heard in my spirit. It was about 2am and I knew he was sleeping but I also knew that my text would be the first thing he'd see once he opened his eyes. When he woke up, he texted back, "I'll never leave you Neak," that's what he said. A bit of relief came over me, yet my gut told me to brace myself. I got off, went home and showered. I was also in school, working 2 jobs, pushing myself through my days. My mother kept me encouraged. She always did.

On February 2nd I received a message on Facebook from a Jessica Lynn. It read, "Your husband is cheating on you with a woman that work at the Supermarket. I'm not sure but I think her name is Sonya. You're welcome." I was sitting in class when I read it, I became nauseous as hell. Scared too. After class I went straight to that grocery store, which was about 5 blocks from my home. Every female in there was hideous. Oh my God, there was no way this was true. Later that day when my husband came home, I just simply asked him.

"Are you cheating with a girl at the grocery store?"

"No! wow," he replied, looking at me as if I was crazy.

"DO NOT LIE TO ME! I shouted, So, you mean to tell me someone picks you two to lie on?" I argued.

"Well Neak, I'm not doing anything," he mumbled in disbelief.

An hour later I called Victors niece to find out who this Sonya was. She was his niece, but she was faithful to me.

"Oh my God, I know Sonya, are you serious, he's having an affair with that ugly thang," gasped Mara.

Mara then found her profile, got a pic and sent me a screenshot. I started to tremble. She was ugly as hell, it hurt me even more. I sat down on the side of my bed, stomach sick and I'm whispering to God he better not let this be true. I got myself together, sent her a message asking her was she having an affair with my husband. She too denied it, saying all she does is speak when she sees my husband. I didn't believe either of them. I braced myself and I kept my eyes open. I still went to work and school with each passing day. Some nights I'd go home on my 3rd shift lunch which was at 3am. I was trying hard to connect the dots. I didn't see anything.

On March 27th I got a message on Facebook from a Jessica Lynch, explaining to me how her husband has told her about my husbands' affair with Sonya. Jessica Lynn now a Jessica Lynch. I'm not out in the public enough for anyone to care to tell me about my husband's infidelity. Clearly this was Sonya. Later that night we had guests at our home, it was about 9pm. I didn't ask my husband about the message I had received earlier that day but I'm sure he and Sonya had been speaking with each other. I acted as if I was tipsy, asked him if I could use his phone because mine was dead. Without thinking he handed me his phone. I was talking silly to our guests heading to the bathroom, giggling. As soon as I got in the bathroom, I went to his text messages. The first message, an unsaved number, asking him "can you talk." I stormed out of the bathroom back into the living room and kitchen where everyone was.

"Victor who is asking you can you talk?" I trembled.

"Why are you going through my phone?!" he shouted.

"Is it her, that ugly girl, its true isn't it?" I began to whimper.

"Well Neak, yes, it's true, I'm cheating," he said so boldly in front of everyone. Moments later everyone began to leave, some hugging me, showing their concern. My friend Amy wanted to scream but Eric made her get in the car. When everyone left, I grabbed my phone and called Sonya.

"Leave my husband alone, don't text his phone anymore, he's married," I explained.

I was so upset, I crawled in bed. Victor left but returned about an hour later. I cried myself to sleep. The next morning, I woke up and went straight to Sonya's Facebook page. Her status read, "He said it's cool, I can keep blowing his phone up."

I called Victor screaming, "*You did not tell this girl to continue contacting you,*" I cried.

"Yes, I did because I wanted to." Victor said so heartlessly.

I hung up the phone, sat there in tears. I Called my mother and asked her to pray for me, as usual, she did. I guess 18 years of marriage was enough for Victor, the journey had come to an end. Hours later our son peeped in my bedroom. He came in and hugged me saying everything was going to be okay. He was good to me. Sweet, respectful young man. Our daughter was living in Virginia. She called me constantly asking me was I okay. I begged her not to worry. Later that night I was scheduled to work. Victor was standing in the bathroom looking in the mirror. I walked down the hallway and stood at the bathroom door.

"We're married Victor, we've been married a long time and we've been through everything together, can you please stop this," I said softly.

"I'm happy doing what I'm doing, I'll stop when I'm ready," he replied with no remorse.

I texted my boss at my 3rd shift job and told her I quit. She texted back "Are you sure?" I didn't respond, I kept begging Victor not to leave that night. Eventually he agreed. Soon we went to bed. I laid there pouring my heart out to him. Sex came about but it was the hurry up and get it over with sex. Hell, I don't even know if that's the name of it but that's what I'm going to call it. The fire was gone. The next morning, I prayed. I called my mother and asked her to come over. She did. She anointed my head with oil and asked God to guide and strengthen me. She tried so hard to cheer me up. She began to play the song Jesus walks by my favorite Artist. I giggled, "Mom you don't even like that man." "I know you love him though Denethia," she replied. My mother did anything she could to make me smile. For hours she encouraged my spirit. I just laid there on the couch, tears falling from time to time. "I guarantee you when you get up from this you will not be the same," my mother said as she slowly walked out the door. Hours later Victor came home, showered and left. He didn't stay home that night. I got up the next day, dragging myself to work. He told me to leave him alone, he told me to move on. I was at work crying on my co-worker shoulder. "We can go beat her ass Neak, come on," said my co-worker. I smiled with tears still coming down my face. I wasn't going to do anything to get in trouble. I had made it to age 36 with a clean record after all the hell I had been through over the years. I wasn't about to mess it up. Especially not over Victor. I was so weakened. I even got switched over to 1st shift on my 2nd shift job, you know what Victor said to me, "I hope you don't think that's going to change anything because it's not." He was so cold. Just like that Victor walked out on me. No, it wasn't just like that, he had to have been having an affair with this woman for some time and I'm not talking a couple of months. Twenty-two years married for 18 of those years and now he won't even text me back. Eventually, our son moved out with his girlfriend. Victor wasn't staying home at all. He'd come shower, stay about an hour then leave. Sometimes he didn't come home at all. He was puffed up like he had a Supermodel on his arm.

His words cut my soul so deep. I'd ride around all night looking for his truck. I'd call my dad and cry. He'd say, "Denethia, you'll be one hell of a woman when this is over." My dad always reminded me that God was with me. I loved him for that. After driving all my gas out I'd go home and cry myself to sleep only to get right back up and push myself to work. Some days I'd call out. I just didn't have the strength. I told God not to ever allow hurt to rest in my bosom again. There was no pill or song that could pull me out of what I was feeling. I had never died before but this that I was feeling couldn't have been far from it. My flesh weighed down on my bones. A crushing to my spirit. I wanted death but I did not utter those words. One night I asked Mara to ride with me. We were listening to music, laughing, having a good time. It made me feel a little better. Returning to my home I saw the back of Victor's truck at the general store in our neighborhood, so I went and pulled up beside him. A little girl was sitting next to him. "Neak that's Sonya's daughter," explained Mara. Seconds later Sonya came out of the store wearing her pajamas, glanced at me and smiled, then went and got right in my husband's truck. Victor had the look of don't kill us on his face.

"It's over Auntie," whispered Mara, just let it go". Victor pulled off and I pulled off behind him. He kept straight at the tracks, I made a right and went home. I cannot believe I just saw him with that woman. It hurt so bad, yet I had no choice but to be done. It was like in an instant I did not see him the same just by seeing him with her. I went home, laid on my couch. A tear fell down my face because my birthday was at midnight. Moments later Victor walked in put $60 on the counter, said happy birthday, then left back out.

I got rid of my bed. I wanted everything new. All I had in my bedroom was my dresser for my clothes and a few clothes in the closet. Victor began to look disfigured to me. It was like demons had really taken over my husband. I had a couch and a TV. Everyone was gone. One night I cried asking God what in the world had I done to deserve this loneliness. Some nights I was afraid because I never had to sleep alone. I'd wake up panicking, in pure fear but moments later I'd ask God to put his arms around me and protect me. It seemed like the house was creating sounds I had never heard before. I'd be so scared. For years there was always a small crowd at my home. Now it was just me. All alone and afraid. One day Sonya drove up to the stop sign right in front of my home. Victor and I were standing by his truck in our driveway and he looked and saw her, a smile came across his face. I was disgusted. She sat there. I should have shot her. I probably would have if I'd had a gun. I went inside and grabbed my pen and pad. Moments later Victor came in, showered and left. It was just me and God in that house, but God was quiet. I ate egg sandwiches for an entire week once. My money was really tight now. Considering just months before I was the one lending to people. It felt good knowing I could help those around me. That's why I worked so much. Even if Victor wasn't the one lending, I still included him saying "We" did it. I thought I was doing everything as I should. If I was working too much, he should have told me. That's what marriage is about, communication. One night I woke up, instantly the pain rushed my mind and body. I cried out asking God to stop it. I was so scared. I couldn't move, on my couch looking up at the ceiling. I stayed up all night, some moments, pacing the floor. Walking from room to room remembering all the memories we had made in this house. As soon as day came, I called my mother. "Tell God exactly what you want Denethia," my mother expressed. I did just that. I even went to church the following Sunday, looking around watching others praise and worship God. I'd just sit there. Wondering when I was going to have the joy that they had. When was I going to be able to smile again? Sonya posted a picture of her and Victor at the beach. A married man, just living his life with another woman. I sat there on my front porch and cried when I saw that picture. As long as we had been together. Just like that he was gone. I was enraged. I emptied what clothes and shoes he had left in the garbage outside. All of his tools that I could carry I took them to the end of the road. Later that night he came home placing everything back. "You can't just put me out of my home Denethia," Victor said.

"GO LIVE WITH HER," I shouted, "Why do you keep coming here, to rub it in my face, we don't lay with each other why do you keep coming here?"

He left.

The next day Victors oldest daughter and a friend of hers came over. We were sitting on the porch talking. She showed me great sympathy. She said she just didn't understand it. I explained to the children that the situation going on between Victor and I was just that and that they shouldn't feel any anger or ill feeling towards him. When I said Sonya's name, the young lady that was with his daughter said, "Sonya! from the grocery store, with the 3 kids."

I said "yeah, you know her."

She said, "Yeah, I know her, she lives right around the corner."

I gasped, "Girl are you serious?"

"Yes ma'am I am, she's right around the corner."

"Show me," I said.

We got in my jeep and made 2 turns. It wasn't even a whole minute and we were approaching Sonya's apartment. As we approached, I could see Victors truck in the back yard by a fence. I felt so stupid. All those nights I was driving all over the city he was right across the park, 4 houses down. I was ashamed. Humiliated. He stopped by the house later that day I almost threw up in my mouth. He didn't stay long. Of course, he just showered and left. I felt robbed and I was sick of seeing his face. All those years we had encouraged each other. All those years we raised and struggled with those kids. He leaves me for a girl with 3 younger kids, after ours are grown. He began to look stupid to me and I felt stupid for all the times I begged him to stay. It was time I pulled myself up. I remember whispering to God that I wanted peace and prosperity, now I felt like shouting towards Heaven. God you've got to hurry up and give me an even better life after this. This anger that I had, became fuel to pull on God even harder. I'd feel thankful some days, other days I'd feel defeated but each day I talked to God. My mother wouldn't allow me to slumber in doing so. My dad booked me a flight to Dallas Tx to see him. I had never got on a plane before. The experience of boarding a plane was exciting. Catching a ride in the air with complete strangers. I got on and placed my duffle bag above my seat. I sat by the window. Moments later a Caucasian lady came and sat next to me. She smiled. I smiled back. Once the plane began to move slowly, preparing to get in line for takeoff. I turned to her and said, "Excuse me, this is my first time flying and I'm scared, please hold my hand." She smiled and held my hand and with the other hand she rubbed the top of my hand telling me everything was going to be okay. When the plane began to pick up speed, she spoke comforting words to me, still rubbing my hand. I thanked God for that lady. A complete stranger, taking the time out to comfort me. When the plane went up into the air it felt as if I was being pulled out of myself. The lady assured me everything was okay. She was so kind. Once we got in the air, I was calm, I slowly let go of her hand, I thanked her. She pulled out a magazine and began to read. An hour later I pulled up the window shade and it looked amazing. Above the clouds. It was so beautiful. The Sun was so beautiful. I'll never forget that experience. I'm sure it won't be my last. I enjoyed the landing. It was exciting. My dad was so happy to see me and I felt the same to see him. I was there for 3 days. Each day my dad tried to get me to drink beer at 9 in the morning. He was hilarious. He took great care of me. He treated me like I was a little girl. It felt good. It felt really good. He encouraged me to be happy. Explaining to me that I was strong enough to live a happy life all by myself. He also explained to me that if God allowed a man to come into my life, he should only be there to help me grow, make me smile and to bring *more* happiness. He put emphasis on more. I understood. I understood that my happiness was my responsibility. When I got back home, I felt a little higher, a little stronger.

June came, I was lying on my couch rubbing my arms, touching my face. I had no one to do it for me. I just wanted to feel alive. I guess I should have been cheating too, that way I would have had someone to rub my back as my tears fell. I had no one, nothing but silence. I'd pray asking God for direction. It was like I didn't know who I was. I'd work and come straight home, read, sit in silence or listen to music until 6am the next morning when it was time for me to go to work again. I wanted life, no hurt, a best friend and a whole lot of money. I got a call from my Therapist one day as I laid in the middle of my living room floor. "Mrs. Wright, in April your prescriptions were to be refilled, why haven't I seen you?" Heather explained in her country accent. It hit me instantly. The minute I stopped sleeping with Victor I didn't need those pills anymore. I sat up and began to tell Heather all that had happened. "You see Mrs. Wright, all those stories you told me about all the hurt that was connected to him, you can let it go now, forgive them, forgive yourself and start your life. Who are you Mrs. Wright, or should I call you that name anymore? Everything that you want to be, fill your mind with it," explained Heather.

As soon as she hung up the phone I got up, found those pills and flushed them. I was going to break every spirit. Every spirit that I had come in contact with because of Victor. I was going to make myself new, but first I wanted to make myself laugh. I posted a picture of Sonya on my Facebook page saying, "If you want your d*ck sucked for free go down to the Supermarket." My Facebook friends laughed all they wanted. It was funny to me. It even made me feel a little better. About 30 min later I was sitting outside having me a drink. Sonya pulls up to my mailbox, screaming a bunch of nonsense. I ran out towards her, she jumped back in her jeep and I picked up a brick and threw it. Oh, I was mad now, that's an automatic ass whooping. You don't come to no one's house and not fight. I gathered about 5 bricks and my big stick I had behind my bedroom door. I was gone beat her ass silly. I drove around about 10 min then I spotted her pulling up to a stop sign right across the tracks. When she crossed over the street, I turned my jeep around quick as hell and got behind her ass. Hanging all out my truck because my damn windows didn't come down. Yelling, "stop the truck Bitch, stop the damn truck". She got to another stop sign I hopped out and threw one of my bricks but missed. I was gone kill this hoe. She sped off, I closed my door and went behind her. She got to another stop sign. I stopped, jumped out and threw another brick. This time I hit her truck, it wasn't major, just a little dent. She sped off so quickly. I called her ass through Facebook. Laughing, telling her ass not to ever talk tough to me again because we both knew the truth. There was no one there to break anything up. If she was bad enough to pull up to my home, she was supposed to swing. I made it back home, calmed myself down. About an hour later I drove by the magistrates' office and she was coming out. Damn, this hoe trying to make me catch a charge. The next day I went to the magistrates' office because I knew they had my name and I didn't want anyone picking me up from work. I signed a paper and went straight to the lawyer's office. That Lawyer costed me $600. Weeks later we were in court. I was placed on probation. I had to get her truck fixed. That was $485. I went ahead and paid it off weeks later. My mother looked at me and said, "Enough." Victor came by explaining to me that he wasn't going to help me pay for my probation, unaware that I had already paid everything off. But I reminded him of the time that I paid his probation off years ago. I looked his silly looking ass in his eyes and told him I didn't need him. I felt so much better. I was surprised I was on probation. I didn't feel like a criminal. My Lawyer said he would get it deferred and dropped considering I'd never been in trouble. I was happy about that.

In and out was Victor. Walking around like he was superman and I'm here on probation. I was having conversations with other men. Trying to sort out which one I wanted to spend time with. The day came when I decided to do so. I was home, just got out the shower, getting dressed. Victor came in, asked me where I was going, I was shocked. "How in the world do you care Victor," I asked. He sat down on the couch as I finished getting dressed. Minutes later I grabbed my purse and left. I had a wonderful evening. Drinks and laughter. For years he wanted me, I kept telling him no. Well not tonight. I enjoyed his company. I got home about 11pm. I walked in and Victor was still sitting there. "So, where have you been Denethia," He asked. "Victor we're not in position to have a conversation as such," I explained. I walked down the hall to the bathroom and Victor began yelling and screaming all sorts of nonsense. "Is this even happening right now? Victor what in the world is wrong with you?" I asked in confusion. He screamed. "Just shut up Bitch, you Bitch," then rushed towards me. He beat me to the floor. Strangled me. I just knew I was going to die. He kicked me in my head. He shouted as he tore my dress from my body. I was silent and helpless. I crawled down the hall and he took his keys and lashed them across my back. "Just leave," I cried, "Just STOP." He took my phone and broke it before he kicked me once more, then he left. I quickly slipped on a dress and ran to my neighbor's house as fast as I could and called the police. Moments after the police arrived Victor was pulling back up in the driveway. I was sure he was coming back to kill me had those officers not been there. He got out of his truck and the officers asked him what had happened. He told them then they took him to the magistrates' office, I followed. While we were waiting to be buzzed in, he looked at me as he stood there in handcuffs and said, "I guess you're happy now." I looked at him and said, "I'm just trying to be as happy as you are with her." He swelled up but couldn't do anything. We walked up to see the Magistrate. As soon as we walked in the Magistrate says, "Hey, Mr. Wright, what in the world is this, what's going on?" I explained, then Victor explained his side. The magistrate says, "Well, what she's saying is the truth, what do you want to do Mrs. Wright?" I said, "Make him pay for my phone that he broke, he gets paid tomorrow and I know he starts his job at the college on Monday and I don't want to mess that up for him." They all looked at me in disbelief. "Talk to him and tell him not to ever put his hands on a woman again," as a tear rolled down my face, don't lock him up." The officers uncuffed him. The Magistrate looked at me and said, "If he doesn't pay for your phone tomorrow come tell me and I'll have him locked up," The Magistrate looked at Victor and said, "And if he ever touches you again, I'll see that he's locked up for years. Go home Mrs. Wright, we'll talk to your husband just as you asked." I left, went home and laid on my couch. What hate was that. I don't know how long he's been seeing Sonya, now he beats me because I'm tired of being alone. I'm human too, I need attention, affection too. The next day when I got off work $300 was on my kitchen counter. I went and got another phone. I didn't see Victor for an entire week. Then he texted me. Saying how he was sorry and that he didn't know what had come over him. I didn't respond. A couple of days later he walked in, looking remorseful. I didn't fall for it. I didn't accept his apology. I wanted nothing to do with him. He started coming by the house more. I became confused. I thought he loved her. Why wasn't he at Sonya's house like before. "Can we fix our marriage Denethia?" he asked. "Eww, hell no," I responded, I don't want you."

I was over it. I couldn't lay down with Victor ever again and he knew it. He belonged to Sonya now. I went out once more with the young man. I didn't see him again after that. I wanted someone that would light up my soul. I wanted to love. Victor was still coming around, making me sick just at the very sight of his face. I was so tired of him. His words sounded so stupid in my ears. Day after day I longed for a special someone to spend my time with. I made sure I stayed out of trouble. I should have been making sure I was going to work. I got fired the very beginning of October. No sweat, I just searched for another job. October 13th I was on my couch arguing with some young man on Facebook. His opinion was what others shouldn't put on Facebook. My opinion was it was none of his business. Of course, I took it personal. The entire time I had been going through hell with Victor it was my Facebook friends who kept me encouraged. They made me laugh, I made them laugh. I had conversations with women whose husbands had left them as well. They told me their stories. It made me feel better about mine. One lady said her husband left her while their kids were still young. I became grateful that I didn't have to endure that. Another woman told me how her husband left her with a horrible disease. I hadn't experienced that either. Another woman told me it had been ten years since her husband had left her and she was still angry with him. I prayed to God I didn't hold no hurt. Being grateful pulled me out from under Victors spell. While I was arguing with the young man another young man messaged me on Facebook. He told me how I should never change for anyone. I assured him I wouldn't. He changed my entire mood just by saying that. I didn't argue anymore that day. Later that night he messaged me again and it started from there. His conversation was different. He didn't care that I was different. We talked until 5am the next morning. I went to sleep but once I woke up, we were right back chatting again. I was ecstatic to talk to him. Even though we grew up in the same town we were from two different worlds. We talked all day some days. That smile Phortee' placed on my face could not be moved. We didn't skip a beat. My boss from the 3ʳᵈ shift job I had quit in April had to have been watching my Facebook page because she messaged me one day saying. "I see you're better, are you ready to bring your ass back to work?" I laughed so hard and said, "YES!" She placed me on 1ˢᵗ shift this time, with higher pay. I was feeling better. Victor was coming by, asking me to stop seeing whoever I was seeing. I told Victor not in any lifetime would I do so. I told him to go around the corner where he had found his happiness.

I'd always thought of him as a fantasy, as soon as he would get off work I'd be pulling up in his driveway, no matter the time. Every chance I got I was in his presence. He made me forget I had been chained to Victor all those years and I understood we weren't in a relationship, but at the moment, he was enough for me. My dad explained to me that this was the time in my life where I should just have fun and enjoy the young man's company. "Get to know yourself as well while you're getting to know him," my dad explained. So, I enjoyed his company plus his kisses. Every time I took a shower it felt like every word Victor had said to me was falling away from my soul. My spirit was being lifted. I didn't believe anything Victor said anymore. Not even a simple hello. It all sounded stupid to me. I wanted Victor out of my sight. I packed all of his things and told him to come get them or I was going to give them away to a homeless man. I told him that for an entire week. He didn't believe me, sure enough I put all his things in my jeep and dropped them in one of those bins you see outside the fire station for those in need. It felt good too. Just throwing it all away. He went by the house, seeing his things weren't there anymore he called me screaming, "*Where are my things Denethia?*"

"I told you I was going to give them to a homeless man Victor, you thought I was playing?" I laughed. Then hung up the phone. I went to the courthouse, ran in and asked them what I needed to do to get my husband out of our house. One official told me there was nothing I could do since we purchased the house together. It was his property as well. As I was leaving another official followed me out. He walked me to my jeep. "Excuse me Mrs., has your husband ever put his hands on you?"

"He has," I replied.

"When?" He asked

"In August."

"Well, go to the courthouse in Tarboro, file a protective order, you'll get it," he smiled with assurance.

I went straight to Tarboro, filled out every piece of paper I needed to fill out. Couple of days later a lady called me back and said the judge wanted to see me. She walked me upstairs and into his office. He spoke with me kindly, I wanted to cry, I knew he could tell. "Everything is going to be okay Mrs.Wright, my friends and I are going to see to it," he explained. He told me when he wanted me in court. I assured him I'd be there. The court date was January 22, 2018, my mother's birthday. Now that was funny. I made sure those papers were to be served at Sonya's address.

I stayed clear of Victor. My lawyer reminded me of my court date about my probation. I had forgot about it. I walked in the courtroom smiling from ear to ear. Had my hair done, skin glowing. I was stepping into some kind of victory; I just knew it. I sat there smiling and staring at everyone else. I believed I had the best Lawyer in town, so I knew I was going to be okay. Well second best, His boss was the best. This one was cute though. ANYWAY!! When the Lawyer called my name, I went up smiling I couldn't help it. The Judge said "ma'am, you've been smiling the entire time you've been in this courtroom, it's hard to believe you acted this way in this report." I said, "Sir, I didn't do anything, it was my husband and his girlfriend." Everyone began to laugh.

"Exactly what I thought, nonsense," he said, "well ma'am, just stay away from him and her. You seem like a really happy person, stay that way, I'll dismiss everything, you're free to go."

I thanked him, signed a paper and rushed out smiling. "FREE AT LAST FREE AT LAST," I shouted when I got to my jeep. I laughed at myself and it felt so good. Do you know what I went and did then, I went and purchased me a BED! Brand new sheets, fluffy pillows. I had slept on that couch long enough. I slept so peacefully that night. I was still rushing to my fantasy every chance I got. I was unable to think of anything negative when I was with him. 2017 was very hurtful for me but the ending was the beginning of my healing. Victor left me a note saying he was going to press charges because I had thrown his belongings away. I was anticipating the moment he'd get those papers about the protective order I had against him. When he got them, he was upset and told me they wouldn't give it to me but when January came the Judge said different. The judge also told me to get a lawyer and that he was sure I'd win. Victor was angry but I was so glad.

A couple of days later there was no Victor coming in and out of my presence. Weeks later it felt like my ears were being transformed. My spirit was being emptied. I prayed constantly. It felt like I was learning who I was. Felt as if I was being reborn. My home was peaceful. The aura was peaceful. My mother would come by and pray for me still. I'd go to her apartment as well. I bought plants for my home. I'd walk through my home telling God what I wanted. No arguments, no tension. I'd spend my days reading and writing just as my mother told me to do. Listening to motivational speakers online. I even got a second job. Victor hadn't paid the mortgage for the past 6 months. I explained to the Lenders all I had been through and they showed mercy. 2018 was the first time in my life that I had ever paid on my home all by myself, it felt pretty good. I would think of only what I wanted. Even if my fantasy wasn't for me, I asked God to send someone with a spirit like his. I wanted more of me. More peace, to love myself. I wanted to think better, be better. I wanted to accomplish health in my spirit, in my finances. I wanted a new heart, a clean heart. I wanted a new life. I began to meditate. I even started eating healthier.

March came, I had to see a counselor with Victor for throwing his clothes away. When I got there, I went in, told the Counselor who I was. I sat down, looking around at all of her doctrines she had hanging on the wall. She'd glance up from her computer looking at me smiling.

"You don't look as if you've been through all I've heard," she stated.

I smiled and said, "I'm only going to get better."

Victor came in, she motioned for us to go into the conference room. I sat down on one side and Victor on the other. The Counselor told us all that would be said would be confidential. I smiled. Immediately Victor wanted to talk about how I would bring up things of the past. I assured him that this wasn't a session to get back together and that we were here to talk about his belongings I had thrown away. I told him I would never love him again. It was the truth. I didn't want to be in his presence. It wasn't my fault that I wouldn't let him train me to be stupid. I wasn't going to allow him to think for me, him wanting me to believe his lies. That's what he was upset about and I guess that's why he had the affair anyway. I laughed at him as he tried his best to get under my skin. The counselor fought hard to keep from laughing at me. "It doesn't hurt anymore Victor, I do not care," I told him. He sat there in disbelief. I was done. I wanted my divorce. I asked him to drop the charges against me since I wasn't able to get any alimony or spousal support. I had seen a divorce Lawyer, she explained to me that since I made more money than Victor the only thing, he would have to pay the court was $1. Just so they could say he had given me something. It angered me for a moment. I married this man, helped him raise his 2 kids along with our daughter, only to be left with a mortgage while he goes on trips and outings with his new girlfriend. I let that go too. I just wanted to break away from him. I had given my entire life to survival with him. All I wanted now was freedom. After I explained that to him, he dropped the charges. I smiled still. While we sat there, I assured him I'd divorce him. I assured him I'd be alright. I guess he could see the happiness all over me because he was amazed.

When a woman is set free from a man. She gets her power back and I welcomed all of mine. Even the power I didn't know. I was 15 when I met Victor. Sixteen when I gave birth to our daughter and 18 when I married Victor. I didn't know who I was or what I was capable of. All I knew was what I wanted for my daughter, but now, I was determined to have a new life. I left that office with an even bigger smile on my face. Victor had never seen me smile in triumph before. My victory was me. A year ago, I was begging him to stop the foolishness because we had been together for so long. Now, I was thanking him and realizing all that history didn't matter. Toxic relationships aren't so easy to recognize when you're wallowing in it. In my spirit, I was wishing that Sonya had come along way before she did. I was getting better with each passing day. The weight had been lifted. God came to see about me on many occasions, soon he was answering my thoughts. There were things I'd think and sometimes complete strangers would give to me without me even asking. He had his way of showing me he was right there. I'd wake up and this feeling of overwhelming joy would be all over me. I'd immediately start thanking God. Asking him to show himself to me constantly. I'd ask him to walk wherever I was going to walk that day before I even got there. I'd ask him to protect all of the children, guide my babies, keep them safe. Guard their minds and hearts. I wanted abundance for my children, in all that they did. Whatever curse was over my family, lack of anything, I wanted it destroyed. I reminded God of his servants, my grandmother and mother. I knew he remembered all of their prayers and I was sure I was included in those prayers. I reminded him of his own word. He told me he would never leave me or forsake me and that he would be with me always. So, if you're here with me God then there is no lack. So, I started asking him to give me the thoughts to think myself up out of or into anything I wanted. There was constant conversation. Even walking the halls at work, I'd tell God what I wanted and I'd give thanks as if I already had it. A lot of days I'd rush home to pray, lay in my floor. Thanking him gave me peace, the joy that he gave, the rest. I knew I needed to talk with him every moment it came to my mind. I was so grateful. James 1:5 If any of you lack wisdom, let him ask of God, that giveth to all men liberally, and upbraideth not; and it shall be given him. Well you don't have to tell me twice. Even though I know God had been guiding and protecting me all of my life, providing too. I knew I needed to meditate on him as much as possible. Believing that all that I was asking was already done.

All those years. All the hurt and humiliation that had happened to me. It all began to leave me once I got Victor out of my system and out of my sight. The abusers that I had encountered. Those who attacked my character. I didn't want to be in the presence of it anymore. It all reminded me of a poem I had wrote years earlier. It was entitled "Remodeling my home" 2007. It felt even better to recite it in 2018, because now, I had actually did it.

"Remodeling my home"

I had to divorce depression, said goodbye to pain

Beat up confusion and kicked out the rain

Stress tried to stay complaining everyday

But I said don't look at me again, don't even say hey

Anxiety kept trying to get back in

Along with his company called sin

And gloom thought she still had a room

But I cleaned them all out with the biggest broom

I heard a knock at the door it didn't sound the same

I just knew it was lie coming back to play more games

But when I opened the door peace stood there with ease

And comfort followed, oh I was so pleased

Power called and said he was on the way

And joy sent me a card, I got it on Tuesday

Love, yet it was delayed, was the only one that prayed

Grace pulled up in the finest car

Healing my heart of the deepest scar

Friendship came running, put her arms around my neck

Her brother came too, his name was respect

Mercy was so kind, helping me remodel my home

Got rid of all the trash, now the ugliness is gone.

April came, my mother suffered a massive heart attack, but it wasn't the end. She was out for about two weeks when it happened. We weren't going to pull any plugs. We were going to keep her here just like she had always told us if anything was to ever happen to her. That was her third heart attack. God had been merciful to us. My sister Janice handled everything. I wasn't strong enough this time. I told Janice she had to sign everything. She'd be in charge. My brother handled it like any man would, I guess. This was my first birthday without my mother. It hurt because I knew she would have been the first to call my phone at midnight.

Victor called my phone asking how my mother was. "Call Janice phone don't call me," that's what I told him. Then hung up the phone. I know, it was mean, but I didn't want to talk to him. Even though I had a protective order against Victor I knew he was still coming to the house. My lawn would be taken care of. I knew it was him. He didn't let me see him. I was praying constantly. I didn't have my mother to help me. I'd call my aunt and uncles in Virginia. Anybody that I knew could or would pray for me, I contacted them. As the months went by my mother's health continued to fail. She was awake but her blood pressure would not stabilize, and her blood sugar would drop in minutes.

She was moved from one hospital to the next. We'd work and get to her almost every day. My sister and I would go bathe her. My mother would tell the staff that they didn't have to do it, her children were coming. It was tough but there was no way we couldn't take care of our mother. She had done everything in her power for us all of our lives. Even when we became adults she still supplied when she was able. She had been in a hospital bed for 5 months. She was eager to come home. They moved her to a nursing home. She refused to give up her apartment. All she kept saying to us was that she was ready to go home. We'd take her to her apartment sometimes, just to let her sit there for half the day. Ride her around, get her out of that building, let her get some fresh air. We'd take her out to eat. She'd hardly eat when we'd take her. We just wanted to do the things we did with her before the heart attack. The nursing home where she stayed was about 5 miles from my home, so I saw her at least 4 or 5 days a week. Sometimes I'd just sit there and watch her sleep. Hold her hand and say a prayer. Every time I stepped in her room; she'd act so surprised like she hadn't seen me in forever. I'll never forget the conversations I had with my mother. I went to see her after work one day. She was sleeping. I didn't want to wake her. I just sat there. When she woke up, she smiled like never before. I asked her to pray for me. With what little strength she had she did just that.

"Don't forget to build my church Denethia, whichever one of you can, build my church," my mother said.

"I promise we will," I replied.

"I can't even cry Denethia," my mother stated, "I know what's going on, I've talked to God."

I fought back my tears as my mother fell back to sleep. All she wanted was to come home, but we weren't skilled enough to care for her at home. She just wanted to go to her apartment. When Christmas day came, we gathered around my mother at my home. Her children, grandchildren and her brother. I took her to church the following Sunday, she had a wonderful time.

The morning of January 11th, 2019 my mother's spirit left this earth, I wasn't hurt. I knew I'd miss her, but I also knew she was with God now. I knew my sister was waiting for her and I knew she would never suffer again. I didn't want a sad funeral for my mother. I wanted all of the Bishops, Apostles, Ministers and Evangelists that my mother knew to have a celebration for my mothers' life. I'll never forget the first song the choir sung. 'Sweeping through the city'. I'll never forget it. It felt as if I could see my mother walking the streets of Heaven. Those people knew my mother, those people ushered her body to its final resting place with gladness, with joy. I knew Heaven received my mother. God assured me.

Two weeks later I started making payments to my divorce Lawyer. Victor refused to help me pay for the divorce. It didn't matter to me anymore. I just wanted complete freedom. A year had passed and the protective order I had against him was expired. One day I was standing out on my front porch. Victor arrived, asked me how my day had been. I looked at him as if he should care. He started apologizing for everything. I apologized as well. He said he didn't mean for things to happen the way they did. I said, "yeah, I know." I explained to him that everything happened for a reason. "What reason do you think Denethia?" he asked. "It made me better Victor, our time was up," I said. I explained to him that I didn't hate him, I didn't hate Sonya either. I mean, we can't be friends, but they were free to go. It was like releasing them from my spirit. I couldn't hold the hurt, it would literally hurt me. I apologized to Victor for conversations I had had outside of our marriage before. Victor and I knew we had spoken with other people before, we're human. Then I asked Victor why he couldn't control the conversation with Sonya. All he kept saying was he didn't mean for it to happen the way it did. May 14th, 2019 I was granted my divorce. Victor wouldn't even shake my hand afterwards. The contract had been destroyed. When he left all that had hurt me went with him.

When I was 20, I found out Victor had a son. The child was born before I even met Victor, but he hid the child from me. He said he was ashamed because he had children by cousins. Calvin's wife, Carrie told me about the child, and I told Carrie that Calvin had another female. Surprisingly, Victors family only hated me for that. Two days later Stephanie, Victors sister, came to my job telling me she heard I was supposed to be telling her fiancé' something about her. She never told me where that lie came from. Clearly, she made it up. This was the "attacking my character" part. Insult to injury. I didn't get any comforting words from Victors family about my hurt in the situation, just hate. I was hurt too and now I was being attacked. Of course, I fought back, even in my home, in front of the children. Victors sister Kelly came over, yelling, saying I slashed her tire. I did, but she didn't see me do it. I didn't think I deserved to be attacked so I attacked back. When she came over yelling, I asked her to leave. She says, "do you think I give a fuck?" I can't remember if I hit her or pushed her. All I know is she fell back, and her twin sister Stephanie caught her, then they rushed out. I wasn't afraid. Victor sat in the middle of our bedroom floor and cried that night. Two days later I received a page from a number I didn't recognize. When I got home, I asked Victor if he knew the number, he said it was Kelly wanting to apologize. In no way was that possible. I was 20 years old and these women in their 30's felt the need to come against me. I had done no more than anyone else. They just used that incident against me because they were never destined to love me anyway. I had no family to help me. I wasn't going to bring my two sisters and mother in it. I was strong enough. I had God.

After that it was shade after shade being thrown. One would even pull up in my driveway but wouldn't come in if I was home. Some of their friends stopped speaking to me. Some would walk by me all puffed up, like they didn't notice me. I understood what I was being shown, I knew who I was, and I knew God was with me. They'd act differently towards me when certain people were around. I noticed everything. I didn't need anyone to stand next to me. I was enough all by myself. Penny even went so low as to going along with information she says she obtained from a child. She never told me what child said it but it wasn't hard to figure out. The only children I was around were Victors children and I also knew she wasn't speaking to a child without an adult present. I saw that she chose to go along with it, just by her saying, "I heard what you told Kevin." She didn't ask me did I say anything. She just automatically placed it on me and that automatically gave me the right to stay away from her the rest of my life. I had never argued to be in the presence of anyone and I wasn't about to start. I did what my mother asked. I counted it all joy. I didn't brainwash my own child with "named brand" clothes so where was it figured that I did with other children in my home. I thanked God for it all, kept the faith that God would reward me.

One of Victors cousins told Victor I was hugging another man on the street. I simply saw someone I knew, and I stopped and talked to him. I'm sure we all have done that before. Even if I would have hugged him, it wasn't enough to say a simple hug meant more than a simple hug. The humiliation, it made me regret being married to Victor. It made me regret Victor being my daughters' father. They'd act as if I was losing because I didn't have their support. Them rejecting me was a show for the world because my daughter didn't have their support either. I had never asked them to help me mold my daughters mind, Dr. visits, school, direction or anything. I had that; I had my mother. After 5 years of taking care of Latasha's children as if they were my own. She was on my phone yelling in my ear as if she had to know me. Acting as if she was saving her daughter from me. I was just like Ike Turner in that movie when I started raising those kids, "What I'm gone do with two more kids." I always told Victor it wasn't fair but at the same time, those were his kids and he wasn't going to let the system take them. So, I stood by his side. I'll never forget those silly words, "You know he love me Neak I'm his baby mama." He had four, so I guess he loved all of us, so what made her feel special, hell, I was the one raising his kids from her womb. Clearly, she hadn't thought that statement through. She acted as if Victor had to be around to witness her saying these horrible things to me. A devised plan to make me look stupid by criticizing me but no one was devising a plan to help her become a better person to take her children and raise them. She couldn't make me look stupid with her responsibility, so I listened. She even told me Victor said I was the one that had took child support out on her. I was, but I couldn't understand how she was angry about it. I wish she would have said just how much she was paying for the listeners to hear that too. Just because I had married Victor her responsibility did not become completely mine, but it did, as if she was dead or in jail, unable. Accepting someone's children is one thing, actually raising them like they're yours is another. Whatever decisions she was making in her life was not my fault and it wasn't up to me to pay for it. She wasn't the one going to the schools for her children, the laundry, when they got sick. It was Victor and I. I guess everyone needed their moment to attack me. I didn't need to hurt her with words. She was already hurting. I could tell because she was focused on destroying me. I don't believe in tearing anyone down, but she was more than happy to try and hurt me. It was like hearing someone scream at you because of their choices in their life. I raised her kids the best I knew how, and I think I did a great job and she found joy in trying to mock me over the phone. I couldn't let any of the foolishness move me, I understood I had my own daughter to look after. No woman could support or provide for my daughter like I could. NOBODY! There was never a conversation about my daughter and I within that family. Nobody ever asked me how anything made me feel. All I ever heard were opinions and criticism. When I told Latasha I didn't want her calling my home anymore she says, "Neak you got to talk to me, you take care of my children." "No, I don't take care of your children anymore," I smiled. "Well I guess

I'll get my kids then," she said as if she'd hurt me. She didn't hurt me, she hurt Victor. She left Kevin though. How do you take one child out of the "hell hole" as she tried to portray and leave the other? I wasn't provoked to violence. I was provoked to pouring into people who appreciated me. Someone had nerve enough to say, "How could you turn your back on his child." There was no way anybody could use a child to control me. My time was up with that and I was more than happy to slide to the next part of my life. I did more than enough. I never heard anyone scream at Victor about hiding kids, I had never heard anyone yell at Latasha about not taking care of hers. Yet I was attacked just by being in those kids' lives and it wasn't my fault that those children were in my home. My mother told me to write. So, I wrote. If you're aware of what abuse looks like you won't think twice about walking away. Abusers will try to kill your spirit to control you; make you stay in their world and if they put you down long enough with words, they can make you kill yourself. Walk away. Just because someone is nice and pleasant to you. They could be a demon in someone else's life. In private. I wasn't the bad guy. People tried to make me out to be just to cover their own short comings. I gave my space, my patience, compassion, time and money. Nobody gave me anything but stupid words. Victors cousin looked at me some time afterwards and said, "I can't believe we believed them," referring to Latasha and her daughter. Like they had made a big mistake in going along with the foolishness. Believing is support. It's not what you do but how you do it. They laughed because they thought they were destroying me. I laughed because I knew parenting does not end and they were the ones who had freed me of my duty. Latasha was the only one who could fire me from that job. I was free to go. Thankful that I walked away. The child Victor hid from me was the only child he put through college, I found that to be so rewarding to that child. God did that. I laughed all I wanted. Had I let any of that hurt cause me to cause harm to anyone I wouldn't have been able to be there for my sister Lashanda. Taking her back and forth to her Dr appointments. I wouldn't have been able to be there for her children. Mara and her children. I wouldn't have been able to be there for my mother. Nobody cared about my life, my mental health or my well-being. I didn't think they cared about my daughter either, so I pushed my daughter to go out into the world. Wherever she wanted to go I supported her. When she'd travel, she'd send me pictures and I'd get excited because I was seeing through her eyes. I encouraged her to learn as much as she could and whenever she'd learn something new, she was more than happy to share the information with me. I wanted my daughter to have complete freedom, didn't want her to be stuck in the opinions of a lot of people. I wanted her sharp, so sharp that her decisions could not be changed by the opinions of others, not even mine. I wanted her well-spoken and firm with her words. I wanted for her, everything that I had ever imagined for me. I was her mother, who was going to take care of her better than me. Most of all I wouldn't have been able to support my grandson. My most prized.

Years later, Penny's daughter sent her nudes to Victors phone and they tried to make me think and feel like I was wrong and that it wasn't true. Her nudes. Four different pictures coming to his phone on the same day they were in the same building and I'm the one that's crazy. I believe they felt since it was only me on my team, then I wouldn't win. That wasn't true. God was with me. That hurt I encountered from them only made me tough. Tough as in the ability to stand alone and still believe in whatever it is that I'm believing. Ella criticized me in private while I was hurting about that. That only taught me to never trust her again, but she ran up to me in public weeks later and hugged me. I understood that that was just for a few people to see. Hell, she could have hugged me when I came to her hurting but treating me like my heart and mind didn't matter was laughter to them. Every time they treated me like I didn't matter only confirmed that I was valuable. I'm sure whatever Penny's daughter had to say about me, Ella sat right there and listened. All of the garbage that I had witnessed through those years, the spirit of it all went out the door with Victor. I didn't hear the redundant question of was I mad because I was off work anymore. Who in the hell sits in anger because they're off work? As hard as I work. I saw a lot of foolishness while connected to Victor. Big dumb man raising his voice at me because he didn't like the way my face was looking. I guess he thought he was embarrassing me. He didn't even speak; he just goes into yelling about how my face looks. I never called him to talk about my heart. I never asked him to sit and comfort me all the years I had been married to Victor, so why does he get to criticize what I look like. Everything that came with Victor left my spirit when he left. Even in 2019 Calvin told me nothing good would happen for me. THE DEVIL IS A LIE!!

My own blood even had nerve enough to tell me they'd make my life a living hell if I didn't show respect. Who in the world did I owe? That was just days before I buried my mother. Clearly not everyone was aware of all I've been through. Why did people feel the need to control me, bully me, humiliate me? It has always hurt because I don't treat people this way. So why is it done to me. Everyone is gone, except Kevin. He is my son. If he loves me, I'll love him. When he wants to go, he's free to go. I hold no prisoners. Majority does not rule, not over me. I looked at it as God taking everyone away who wasn't for me. Those who clearly have no purpose in my life. When I was 25, I spent so much time alone asking God why, but as I grew older, I started asking him when, when was my next move. I rejoice when people reject me now, because I understand and I'm exceedingly glad. No matter what I went through I understood I knew how to create. I was sitting at work one day, realizing that my name wasn't what my foes wanted to be of me. I wrote my nickname (Neak) about 100 times on a piece of paper and I began to think about just what I stood for. I was loving, I was kind and I cared for people. I wanted freedom for people. The next day, same thing, over and over I wrote my nickname (Neak). Hours later I said to myself what can (N) stand for. Whatever the word was it had to be uplifting, because I was full of life. I'd speak life to people even though people had always tried to kill my spirit all my life with their words. I loved laughter, I loved feeling good. I've always wanted everyone connected to me to be blessed. I wanted life for my people. That (N) became Nurturing: The information given from those who had nurtured me was more valuable than any negative word spoken over my life. I remembered how I poured into my daughter, any child that had come in contact with me, I always complimented them because I knew a child would never forget who made them believe. Even as an adult, we still need to be nurtured. We still need hugs and to know that someone cares. Even if no one around you cares, there are people on this planet that do. There are people with information that can lead you to thinking better for yourself. Is that not nurture? It is. The (E) became Empowering: Ever wonder why teams need Cheerleaders, well it's not just their beauty, it's the encouraging words that they bring to their teams. To be surrounded by others uplifting you and giving you the encouragement that you need. That right there can work miracles. To have someone saying, "YOU CAN", even when you feel like giving up. Words build, the right words enlighten and empower. Most need encouragement daily, some most of the time. There are some that are strong enough to empower themselves. Lift your voice and be an encouragement to someone every day of your life. Words to help others and yourself believe that we can overcome and get to the next level of life. Uplift daily, that's the plan. This I know for a fact, you already have "EVERYTHING" you need. The objective is to bring it OUT!! The (A) became Awareness: Once I became aware of certain situations my mother would ask me one question. "What are you going to do about it now that you know about it Denethia?" I'd think about how and why it came to make me better. What could I get from it? I've always been aware of how people spoke to me. Were they speaking life or death? Where they there only when it was beneficial to them? I knew when I became aware of anything in my life that made me feel enslaved, I could change it. There are people that are afraid, drop the fear. You are not alone. When you're able and aware, you can acquire. The (K) became kindness because I was kind.

Simple compliments go a long way. Telling someone they can, encouraging others. A simple smile to or from a complete stranger. Helping someone, uplifting someone. We don't know the entire stories of one another, so when we come in contact, the smallest act of kindness can pull someone through their day. Even if they don't see your face for the rest of the day. Even if they never see your face again, they'll never forget how you made them feel in that moment. Let it be kindness.

I created N.E.A.K in 2014. I was proud to do so because I knew who I was and I still know who I am.

Whatever happens to me, I'll pull life from it. Romans 8:28 And we know that all things work together for good to them that love God, to them who are the called according to his purpose. I'll always believe that what came to harm me came to help me, it's an appointed time for victory. I'll just keep being still, knowing that God is God. Now, I spend my days alone thanking God. Thanking him for all of the lessons and blessings. Sometimes I wonder was I really that special to God to have had parents that I've never heard argue with each other. Not once had my mother ever spoke bad about my father and when I'd hear my father speak of my mother he'd say, "she's right, whatever she is saying, she's right." They'd teach me but God was the main reference. My mother would make me read the bible whenever I'd get angry. I remember sometimes I'd go to my mother crying and all she'd say is "Read." I'd cry even harder. Sometimes I'd call my father, telling him everything and he'd give no feedback, all he'd say was talk to God baby. God was with me the entire time and every day I'd wake up speaking with him. All through my day I'm asking him to be attentive to me, my life is better this way. He explained to me why things happened the way they did, and I was right. He wanted me all to himself. For his purpose. Since Victor left, I love myself even more, I value myself more. My time, my mind, everything that's mine, is just more valuable to me.

Work and meditation, that's all I had. Of course, I'd write, that's what I loved. Oh yeah, I had YouTube. I loved those motivational speakers. Any kind of information I wanted it was there. The encouraging words were amazing. Anytime I needed a good word, I'd get online and listen to these people. These preachers. I loved them all. It felt like hearing words from big brothers and sisters I had never met. To hear these men and women speak, I felt it was all just for me, at the right time.

Law of attraction, are you serious? Well, it's true because I knew what I wanted in 2017 and in 2019 I was still being changed from the inside. I thought and meditated on what I wanted. I prayed and believed. I spoke life over my life. "Life and death are in the tongue," my mother would say. I'd read that bible, over and over. Even if I felt bad, I'd think of something silly to make me laugh. Laughter had been like a dose of medicine all my life, but I knew God was the answer to it all. I needed to feel good. I didn't hate Victor, but everyone was confused about me. Everyone wondered how in the world was I happy. I wanted to be happy.

Sonya got upset with me because Victor told her friend he wanted to come home, but I wouldn't take him back, so she attacked me on Facebook. I couldn't get mad; I was so happy. Whatever Sonya was going through with Victor was her business and whatever Victor was feeling was his. I wanted no parts of it. I asked him to stop telling people we use to be married. I didn't feel proud to honor something that was over. The children were raised, and I had nothing but freedom. My bills were paid. My health was perfect. God allowed me to keep my right mind these past 25 years. So many people I knew had died, went crazy, on drugs or dealing with some type of terminal illness. I was grateful. Thankful that the God of all creation had given me the ability to be a better person. A loving person, even though people tried to kill me mentally. God gave me life after all I had been through. I had never been this happy in my life and I didn't have a man to call mine. I had no title. Only my name, Denethia. I'd walk through my home telling Denethia how much I loved her and how much I was proud of her. So much goodness is coming for you Denethia. I also reminded Denethia that God had been with her before her grandmothers' grandmother was born. I reminded Denethia that she was an heir to the Throne of the Creator, the Source, The Father. I'd also walk through my home thanking God for sparing my life. I could be anything in the world I wanted to be. All I had was me and I was more than enough. I want to encourage others. I really want others to know that even if everyone around them is against them all they have to do is keep believing in themselves. Depart from those people who mentally, verbally or emotionally abuse them, that's not love and I'm sorry doesn't mean a thing. The same people encouraging you to forgive can be the same people orchestrating your hurt. Don't ever think you're beneath anyone, we all matter. Being planted around certain people sharpened me. God saw what I needed. It hurt but I made it through. People would look at me crazy whenever I'd say I don't hate Sonya. I don't.

I thank Sonya, so much. I wasn't aware of who I could become. Who I could experience and love. Where I could go. Sonya helping Victor destroy our marriage crushed my soul and made me brand new. I felt so good in my spirit. Sometimes I remember all of the bad things that happened to me, but it doesn't hurt my spirit anymore. It is forgiven, I'm forgiven. I walk alone but I'm not losing. God is with me. The truth does set you free. It may hurt, you may lose friends, but it opens doors to new beginnings. This life is a journey. We've all been to a funeral, so we see the only way out. Everyone won't be there all the time. Everyone isn't meant to stay. We experience. That's how I see everything now. We experience things and each other and we learn. I didn't lose value when Victor left me, instead, God gave me more of him. I am my Throne. Any information that helps you grow, pass it along to help another. I do believe we spark each other.

I visit my mother, sister and Grandmother once a week. I work hard, very hard. I want to live. I want to meet new people, different people. Even though I've made a difference in someone's life I want to make a difference in somebody else's. I want to really be loved. I will one day. I asked God for my fantasy, but if he's not the one God send his twin. I'll wait. I didn't feel the need to guard my heart because I wasn't afraid. The thought of loving him was too strong. I was certain I'd be satisfied just to be in his presence. I didn't measure him by his material possessions but by the way he made my spirit feel. I was so open, and it felt so good. I couldn't remember a time I had ever felt this way. It felt new. Any hurt that I had was gone. I was at ease, at peace and every moment with him seemed like the first time. I felt so alive, I began to appreciate the simple things. A simple smile or gesture, a simple compliment. A hug. One day I kissed my hands because I was sure there was someone somewhere who didn't have any.

Even in my sin I felt God had sent him. I always believed he allowed things for a reason. Then what reason did he allow him to me. I'd pray he'd stay until I figured it out. I chose to love him. His spirit spoke to mine. It felt I had been awakened; my mind was very clear. It was like I had never known confusion. My heart was willingly open. I'd ask God to protect me just so I could get back to him one more time. Allow me to see his eyes, touch his hands, kiss his lips and hear his words, his voice brighten my entire world. Everything about him brought me peace. His aura was pleasant energy, humble. So humble, yet so loud. I could still hear him speak without his lips saying a word. I felt at home with him as if my spirit had been longing for his and finally found it. It was like rest. His beauty, spirit. I wanted to become better and I knew it all started with the way I thought. Speak better, live better. So many years I took pride in helping others, now all I wanted to do was invest in me. More aware of myself and what I needed. What words could I learn, what words could I speak to my spirit to enlighten my everything.

Meditation, quiet my mind as much as possible. But no matter how quiet I became somehow; I still felt his presence. I wanted the kind of spirit he had. I wanted my words to be few yet powerful. I wanted to learn how to be alone and happy about it. Whatever I could grasp to make me better, I wanted it. Yeah, I noticed, good things happened, Of course, I was blessed. I wanted those I came in contact with to handle me with peace and I the same with them. He changed my spirit without asking or criticizing me and that made him a special kind of rare. I was pleased with it all. He could use his hands but only to stroke my hair. His gentle touch meant everything. His soft kisses were pure energy. I found so much pleasure in pleasing him. I'd keep myself, to myself until he returned. I only wanted his vibe, his mysterious chemistry. I asked God to bless our eyes to see each other in the brightest light that we had to offer. Even if he's not destined to be mine God just let me remember all that he is. When you truly love someone you just don't care to entertain anyone else on any level. With every passing day I'd wake up thanking God then immediately think of him. I'd look forward to his words. I'd look for anything to love about him. His flaws were beautiful to me. There was brand new love from my soul to his with every new day. I'll love Phortee' forever, even if he walked away. It was intimacy without touching me. There was no obligation, no commitment ever established, yet I was his. I held on to everything he didn't say. Kept the thought of expectation in the grave and asked God to grant me power. Whatever word or action I could have displayed to keep him I would have did it. I would have fixed whatever was broken. Whatever had been lost. I just wanted to grow in love with him. The words that came from his lips were sometimes bitter but sweet because they were pure. The art of his honesty. I would whisper his name close my eyes and search for the sound of him saying mine. The minute he'd utter the words I'd be back in his presence. I couldn't find the nerve to tell him no. I'd pray hoping he'd be merciful to my heart because I knew I'd go wherever he says, do whatever he'd say do. All because his spirit calmed me. I wanted his eyes to look into mine and see everything that he thought was love. I wanted to capture it in that very moment. Searching for words to puncture his heart. What touch would have him desire me more. What melody could he hear to think of my spirit. I believed his spirit had found mine in the moment of one of Gods dreams. I felt the intentions were pure. No suffering and the souls are at ease. I love him for him, even the bad I had yet to see. I was ready to forgive it. I only wanted to love him. I had never seen love out of this window. There is no other human with his DNA, his print. Uniquely designed, one of a kind. Humbled with controlled pleasure. Lingering love. I needed it the most, his affection. Always call for me. There was no personality like his yet the insanity in me would search for him in others. I'd still love him tomorrow even if I woke up in another world, with another name, I'd never forget his. Thoughts of him were forever written on my soul. I prayed constantly, for many days. He said he'd get better and he did. I'd accept all that he'd say and each time he delivered. I didn't want to question what type of love this was. I was just thrilled that my heart had been given the opportunity. There was no need for pressure the seed had been planted and nurturing it was my delight. His lips and hands, his aura. It was embedded in me. Like I had knew no other soul. People were swift to kill things that looked like joy to others. I hid his picture in my bible and the love in my heart. If I spoke it would be in parables or a lyric of the greatest Artist of our Era. These memories began in another world and when the creator spoke, they became life. So many days and nights in his arms. I'd dream of him every time I slept next to him. Even in spirit we danced and smiled as if we were in the flesh. He helped take away the hell that had cluttered my mind for many years. It never happened, that's what I'd tell my soul. I'll never forget my friend. Even if I never see him again. I was grateful just to experience him. I was at peace with everything. Especially everything concerning my sister and my mother. Some expected me to cry constantly, give up or be sad. I could only do the complete opposite. I was only grateful. That's all I had ever seen my mother do, give thanks. My sister would do the same. I was Blessed to have the opportunity to experience life with them and accommodate them during their time of transition. I had come across a quote by Einstein, "Energy can neither be created nor destroyed; energy can only be transferred or changed from one form to another." Immediately I thought of my mother and sister. We are energy, our spirits will leave our bodies, but the spirit will never die. That's the way I see it. I've always searched and tried to obtain the things that made me "feel" uplifted, anything to stay in good spirits. Only to find out that my mother had the answer the entire time. I've had the money, the friends in high places. Once all of that faded, I was still empty, still lonely inside. When my sister found out she was sick, we both began to pray daily. We wanted God to heal her so bad. She'd call and pray; I'd call her and pray. I'd get ministers to go to her home and pray for her. Even though they didn't ask for anything I'd give $20 or $30, if just for gas. I'd tell people what time the ministers would be coming to my sister's house and they'd show up too. My sister would thank me. I'd thank her too. She'd say, "why are you thanking me Neak?" I'd say, "Cause these prayers affect me too." We were praying for her health but I'm sure God was touching everyone in the midst concerning situations in their own lives. I'd take my sister to Duke hospital and sit with her the entire time, I didn't mind. I did everything she asked. Our baby sister Janice would do the domestic things around the house, my mother did too. We never complained helping each other. We'd been poor all our lives, once we became adults, working was automatic and if you missed a day Janice was there to see why. If your reason wasn't good enough, she'd say, "We don't have time for the foolishness." Janice took it pretty hard when Lashanda left. They were best friends. One morning Lashanda woke up in the happiest spirit ever. She said she had dreamed that she was in bed and Angels were washing and massaging her body. She said the Angels were so pretty and it all felt so good. When I got to her home later that day she got up and walked to the stop sign by her home. She had never done that. She laughed all day long thanking God. The last time she went to the hospital she got married right there in her hospital bed. Nurses and Drs from other floors in the hospital decorated her room with flowers and attended her wedding. It was about 10 family members. She was so happy. "I got to get out of here, go home and enjoy my husband." Lashanda said, as she grinned from ear to ear. Two days later the Dr's were telling her she wasn't going to be able to go home. "Well, I'm not going to die here, send me to Duke," she said. They airlifted her to

Duke. Two weeks went by, we were back and forth spending days and nights with her. That last Friday she told us she wanted to spend the weekend with her husband and that she would see us Tuesday, she said she had so much to tell us. She told me to bring my pen and paper to write everything down. I got so excited. I was ecstatic to hear what she had to say so I could imagine it all. That Monday was the first day of school for her girls. Her husband made sure they got there. We talked on the phone that day. She made a lot of phone calls making sure everyone would be there that Tuesday. That Tuesday morning, she sent me a message through Facebook. "Good morning Neak, I was so tired last night, my stomach was hurting so bad, I'm good now, I slept all night last night." I told her I figured she was resting by her not answering when I called last night. I called her about noon, she was on the phone with my Uncle. I told her everyone was going to get there about 3 or 4pm. She was fine with that. My daughter was on her way down from Virginia. When she got here, we got on the road to go see Lashanda. About 3:30pm I called Lashanda to let her know we were almost there. The nurse answered her phone. "Hey, is this Lashanda's room," I asked, confused. "Yes, this is her room, the nurse replied, who is this?" "This is Denethia her sister, let her know we're almost there." "Oh, yes, Denethia, has no one talked with any of you?" she asked. "No, no one has talked to me, why, what's up?" I didn't think anything of it considering other family members had been speaking with her all day. "Lashanda expired about 15 minutes ago," The nurse said. "What did she say, what were her last words?" I cried to the nurse. "She said tell all her family that she wants them to live their lives and be happy," The nurse said with deep remorse. "Which one of you were with her?" I asked. "I was," said the nurse, I told her that she was loved, that's all I kept saying to her." I cried and called my mother. They were on the road as well. As soon as I told my mother she began to yell. As soon as we walked into Lashanda's room it's like we could see the peace all over her face. Her daughters didn't take it hard. We kissed her, held her hand and as usual, we thanked God. We sat there for a couple of hours. When it was time to leave, I smiled at my sister because all I could think about was her explaining to those two nurses that were caring for her that they looked like Anna and Elsa from the movie Frozen. Lashanda loved Princesses. "We are Princesses Neak." Lashanda would always say. My mother had even started to call herself a Princess once she kept hearing Lashanda say it. I even became Princess West; I called her my alter ego. The mortician even gave my sister a royal scene for her viewing. People came from everywhere to see Lashanda's body. They said everyone was talking about how pretty she was. Vera fashioned Lashanda, that was her sister-in-law. They even placed a crown on my sisters' head. My mother sung one of Lashanda's favorite songs. I made sure I recorded a little. Sometime later my mother came over to my home, she was hurt. "Lashanda clearly told him not to be with that girl and he is with her anyway," Explained my mother, "Did he even love my daughter, did he even care?" I hugged my mother. Explained to her that Lashanda was with God and any earthly activity going on she wasn't aware of it. "What will we do Ma, tell him who to love, just let it go Ma," that's what I told her.

"It's about respect Denethia," my mother said. "Well his daughters will repay him if it's destined," I explained, there's nothing to say or do Ma, Lashanda is in everlasting peace, there is no husband, boyfriend or boo, only God."

No matter who he loved, I still saw him as Lashanda's husband, I still loved him. He was still Marshonda and Marshayla's father. All was well with me. I just wanted everyone to do as my sister asked. Live their lives and be happy. Happiness is everything. I don't think anyone can function properly purposely living in torment, yet when hurt comes, we manage to push through.

God reminded me of my short comings. He reminded me of everything I spoke to him. He took me back to when I gave birth to Denysia. I was 16 and scared. Scared of raising a child without the father. Scared of not being able to provide for my child. Terrified of her seeing things I had seen. God took me back to my prayer. He even showed me where I was laying when I said it. Denysia only 4 days old, it was dark outside. I told God to allow Denysia's father and I to marry, raise Denysia together, give her everything and send her to college, that's it. Why in the world did I say "that's it" because once we sent Denysia off to college our marriage began to crumble but divorce was never an option. I had never known Victor to sleep with another woman even if he had and vice versa. Victor provided for us as he should have. He is a good man. I can't write his entire life off based on this one incident with Sonya. The incident just hurt like hell, but I understood we were human. God even took me back to the time when I asked him for a child. I said God I want a child with my own blood, and I'll love that child with everything in me. A little over a year later Denysia gave birth to Troy, my grandson. As I was watching the child trying to crawl one day in my living room something spoke to me and said, "well, the child does have your blood." I jumped up and laughed, tears swelled in my eyes. I said God, you are defiantly hilarious. From then on out I was very careful as to how I prayed and when Victor left me, I was more precise. Lay all over me God, Let your peace dwell in me. I want overflow of your goodness. Allow me to forgive quickly. Allow me to smile because of your goodness. Let my mind stay on you. Open Heaven to me. Let me thank you all the days of my life. Save my soul. Tell me where to go. Who to be around? Let everyone I come in contact with handle me with peace and I the same to them. Thank you for my millions God and if that's too small thank you for my billions. I want your joy every day I wake up. Bless the children God. Those who hate me let them know I don't hate them. Let there be no harm to them or me. Teach us God. Sit with us. Heal our hearts. Our lives are spared. Don't allow me to speak evil. Let my words be life. Let my presence be peace. Send me great words and fix my mouth to speak them. Thank you God for mercy, EVERYTHING could have been worse than what it was. I'll be 40 in April 2020; you can take me out of the wilderness now God and I still live and have a flourishing life here on earth. I'm ready to go higher. I'm ready to live my new life. That love that you send me, let him be all that a husband should be to a wife. Let no abuse of any form be in him and I the same to him.

Let us inspire one another. Help each other learn and grow. Laughter, love, joy and peace be between us. When we touch each other let it be honored by you God. Prosperity, prosperity, prosperity in every area of our lives. In Jesus name I came, in Jesus name I pray. Amen.

I know for sure what I'll be doing the rest of my days. Praying, reading and writing. I encourage others to read too. Did you know you could be reading the bible and your mind and spirit could be concluding a decision in another area of your life. You could be reading and instantly figure out where you want to relocate, or what shoes to buy for that dress. How to properly handle a situation that's been boggling your mind for some time.

Do you know why? Because the word of God is living. While walking through my hurt I learned that the hurt is what propelled me to be greater. It taught me to keep record better, write better, pray constantly. I also found out that God allows Satan to work and usually it's through someone close to you. I also found out that no matter how ugly I thought Sonya was it was her spirit that caught Victor's so maybe Victor went to where he saw himself. Just because he left me doesn't mean something was wrong with me. So, I had to ask God for forgiveness for all the mean things I had said about her and he told me to keep in mind that he would repay. He also reminded me that he loves them too. They were his children too. That's how I set it free. Understanding that all of us had sinned. Understanding that we are flesh. Praying will definitely help you forgive people. God designed us to love, especially love him. We've been taught pain is bad. We all know for sure it hurts but when the swelling goes down, everything is alright or it's even better. The pain teaches us, it helps us grow. I'm so grateful to be alive and well and I thank everyone on this journey. The good, the bad and the ugly, God allowed it. Talk to him honey. Don't wait until the hurt come, we need the prayers way before the trial reaches us. God has already worked it out. There is no defeat only growth. Keep that in mind and you won't give up if you stumble. No matter who leaves or who stays, keep in mind that you are your Throne. No one can leave with the promises God has already spoken over your life. You are your Throne. #IAmMyThrone. I am Denethia. When Victor left, I became new. I became better. Thank You.

Thank God, For everything.

Thank you

Mother

Other books by Denthia Wright

In our lives

Kingdom Come

Royalty

What blows in the Wind

Made in the USA
Middletown, DE
27 January 2026

27579171R00085